FENIX AND THE FIREWORK FLIERS
A Dance-It-Out Creative Movement Story

© 2024 ONCE UPON A DANCE Redmond, WA
Illustrated by Scott Partridge, www.jevaart.com
In Collaboration with Author Christine Herbert
Konora Photos in Collaboration with Dan Lao Photography

All rights reserved.
No part of this publication may be reproduced, distributed, or transmitted in any form or by any means, without the prior written permission of the publisher, except for brief quotations for review/promotional purposes and educational/noncommercial uses.

Each Dance-It-Out! story is an independent kids' one-act play ready for the imagination stage.
Fenix the firefly's short wings make it hard to fly fast and join the Firework Fliers. When best friend Bolt eats too much nectar and can't fly, will Fenix find a way to light up the sky and help reveal the *Spirit of the Season*?
Find out in this charming story of friendship, problem-solving, and courage.

Library of Congress Control Number: 2023924222

ISBNs 978-1-955555-82-1 (paperback); 978-1-955555-83-8 (hardcover); 978-1-955555-81-4 (ebook)
Juvenile Fiction: Animals / Insects, Spiders, etc. (Interactive Adventures; Imagination & Play; Performing Arts / Dance)

First Edition

All readers agree to release and hold harmless ONCE UPON A DANCE *and all related parties from any claims, causes of action, or liability arising from the contents. Use this book at your own risk.*

The Dance-It-Out! Series
Tammy the Troll: A Dance in the Forest: A Prop-Based Movement Story
Eka and the Elephant: A Dance-It-Out Creative Movement Story
Dayana, Dax, and the Dancing Dragon (Duplicate Story: Danny, Denny, and the Dancing Dragon)
Brielle's Birthday Ball: A Dance-It-Out Creative Movement Story
Fenix and the Firework Fliers: A Dance-It-Out Creative Movement Story
Belluna's Big Adventure in the Sky: A Dance-It-Out Creative Movement Story
Joey Finds His Jump!: A Dance-It-Out Creative Movement Story
Mira Monkey's Magic Mirror Adventure: A Dance-It-Out Creative Movement Story
Princess Naomi Helps a Unicorn: A Dance-It-Out Creative Movement Story
Petunia Perks Up: A Dance-It-Out Movement and Meditation Story
The Grumpy Goat: A Dance-It-Out Creative Movement Story
Sadoni Squirrel: Superhero: A Dance-It-Out Creative Movement Story
The Cat with the Crooked Tail: A Dance-It-Out Creative Movement Story
Sora Searches for a Song: A Dance-It-Out Creative Movement Story
Freya, Fynn, and the Fantastic Flute: A Dance-It-Out Creative Movement Story
Frankie's Wish: A Dance-It-Out Creative Movement Story
Danika's Dancing Day: A Dance-It-Out Ballet Story
Andi's Valentine Tree: A Dance-It-Out Ballet Story
Daryl and the Dancing Dolls: A Dance-It-Out Ballet Story
Ella's Dance Debut: A Dance-It-Out Ballet Story

Royalties donated to charities through 2030.

Hello Fellow Dancer!
I'm Ballerina Konora.
It's so lovely to meet you.

Dancing brings me so much joy, and I'm excited to share it with you.

Will you be my dance partner and act out the story with me and the creatures? I've included ideas for movements that could match the story. You can decide whether to follow these instructions, use the illustrations, or create your own moves. Get creative by trying different actions next time.

Be safe, of course, and do what works for your body in your space. And feel free to settle in and enjoy the pictures the first time through.

Konora

ONCE UPON A DANCE, the sun shimmered above the horizon as the creatures of Silver Birch Forest flocked to the Solstice Celebration.

The longest day of the year was the perfect reason to feast on spring's bounty of mushrooms, fruits, greens, and nuts. Laughter and delicious smells filled the air as the animals gathered.

The sun shines longer on the solstice. Let's make a round sun shape.

Stand tall like a silver birch. Stretch to the sky and feel your roots reaching down.

Imagine a plate of delicious food. What do you see on your plate? Choose a food, and use your body, arms, or legs to create its shape. You could give hints and let someone guess the food.

The highlight of each celebration was the Firework Fliers, a squad of one hundred fireflies who would light up the sky in a dazzling, darting, dizzying kaleidoscope. The grand finale would reveal the animal who most captured the *Spirit of the Season*.

Only a few knew who would be celebrated until the fireflies revealed the elders' decision with a sparkling picture in the sky.

The bravest and most talented fireflies were chosen to be Fliers. They needed speed to glide high and low, skill to dodge branches, and teamwork to flash their lights in harmony.

Pretend you're a wise elder of the forest. What animal are you? How do you move and speak?

Next, move like a firefly auditioning for the Firework Fliers. Show off your best moves to impress the judges.

Fenix the firefly had dreamed of being a Firework Flier, but shorter-than-average wings made it hard to zoom and twirl. Flying in short hops near the ground seemed a far wiser choice.

Fenix's best friend, Bolt, was a recent recruit to the squad. "I get to be the highest point in the firework finale!" Bolt said, putting on his shiny new Flier's helmet. Fenix gave Bolt a high five, then whispered, "Can you tell me about the finale firework?"

Bolt grinned. "You'll have to wait and see! But watch for me at the tippy top of that tree," he said, pointing directly above.

Jump forward, sideways, and backward like Fenix bouncing low on the ground. Bend your knees at the start and end of your jumps.

Put on your fancy helmet. Pull the strap tight under your chin and tilt your head from side to side to test it.

Try some different high fives: up high or down low with your palm facing different directions.

The gathering creatures settled in the grove. Squirrels opened their stores of acorns. Rabbits brought piles of sweet clover. Bats presented clusters of ripe berries.

"Don't forget, I'm counting on you to cheer me on," Bolt said, admiring the bears' glistening honeycombs. "It won't be as fun without you. But if I can hear you cheering, it will be like you're up there with me."

"I **am** a good cheerleader," said Fenix with a few claps and whoops in demonstration.

"The best!" Bolt smiled. "Oh, look! The butterflies brought nectar! My favorite!"

Scurry like a squirrel. Hop like a bunny. And flap like a bird.

Clap your hands and shout an encouraging message.

Flutter around your space like a graceful butterfly.

"Easy does it, Bolt," Fenix said. "Remember your bellyache from drinking too much nectar at the butterflies' tea party?"

"Too much nectar? No such thing. Besides, I need energy for flying." As Bolt slurped his second helping, Fenix tried to guess which creature would be named *Spirit of the Season*. "A praying mantis? A raven? A rainbow trout?" said Fenix, mimicking their movements.

"You'll never guess. Not in a million years!" Bolt chuckled.

Make sipping sounds by breathing in through your round lips (pretend to sip through a straw).

Bend your elbows and wrists with your hands held high in front of you. Move your head side to side and up and down as far as you can—a praying mantis can look in every direction except backwards.

Lean forward and flap your raven wings in the breeze.

Swish and sway like a fish.

When the sun had cast long shadows across the field, Bolt put down his empty cup. "I'd better join the squad before it gets dark."

He struggled to rise, but his full belly kept him rooted to the ground. "Oof! I should have listened to you."

Bolt flopped backward and groaned. "There IS such a thing as too much nectar."

"Can the show go on without you?" Fenix asked.

"If I'm not up there at the very end, it won't look right. I'm going to be in so much trouble." Bolt moaned and covered his face.

Sit down, then slowly lean or fall backward and rub your full stomach.

Cover your face with your hands.

Fenix looked up to the tippy top of the tall tree, then followed the trunk down, down, down to the ground near where they were seated. It was a long way to the top, but Fenix had an idea.

"I think I can help," said Fenix mysteriously.

"How?" asked Bolt.

"Leave it to me," said Fenix. "Give me your helmet."

Bolt handed over his helmet, and Fenix buckled it and stood tall. "I've got this," he said.

Lift your eyes and chin, and slowly lower them as if you are following the trunk down.

Put on your helmet and strap it under your chin.

Stand up straight with your hands on your hips and give a confident "I've got this."

Fenix hopped to the bottom of the tree trunk.

"Trying to reach the top?" asked a bullfrog. "That's a long way up. Lucky for you, I have strong legs." The bullfrog held out a long, sticky tongue. "Grab on, and I'll give you a boost."

"Thanks all the same, but I have strong legs, too." Fenix flew-hopped up the tree while keeping a wary eye on the frog.

Fenix climbed and climbed until a spider, suspended from a silky web, kerplunked directly in the little bug's path.

Bend your knees and touch the floor. My frog pose makes me want to jump!

Stick out your tongue as far as you can and wiggle it around.

Move while you look backward. For an extra challenge, try shaking your head at the same time. Ooh, that's tricky.

With a few steps toward Fenix, the spider said, "You look weary, my sweet. Why don't you rest? I'll wrap you in a cozy blanket." The spider motioned to some bundles swinging gently in the breeze.

"Thanks," said Fenix, darting to the opposite side of the tree, "but I need to hurry. My friend's counting on me."

After a few more hops, Fenix stumbled upon an owl perched stock still.

Walk on your hands and feet as if you were a four-legged spider (even though spiders have eight legs).

Perch with bent knees and folded wings.

The owl's eyes opened wide and stared directly at Fenix. "'Tis very dark, but lucky for you, I have excellent night sight." The owl snapped its beak open and shut. "If you hop in, I shall fly you, quick as a wink, wherever you like."

"Thank you, but I can light my own way." Fenix glowed and wiggled, hoping to remind the hungry owl that fireflies do not taste very good.

Open and close your mouth as if you are a hungry owl snapping your beak at your next meal.

Shake your hips from side to side.

The little firefly climbed bit by bit toward the treetop.

The crowd below chattered with excitement as the Firework Fliers (minus one) gathered. Then, the audience burst into applause as ninety-nine fireflies flashed their lights and began the show.

Climb with your arms and legs. Start by reaching/lifting your opposite arm and knee. Then try using the same arm and leg. Which feels best?

If you're with other people, try to clap at the same time by watching each other. See if you can do it ten times in a row.

The Fliers spread, circled, spiraled, and flickered their rhythms.

The animals leaned in, excited for the upcoming big reveal.

Who would be named *Spirit of the Season*?

Fenix climbed faster.

The ceremony included highlights of past years' winners. The fireflies assembled in a rippling band of light to create the image of a garter snake.

The grass rustled as the watching snakes slithered in appreciation.

Spin like a dancing firefly.

How fast can you climb?

Lie on your belly to slither like a snake. Move your head from side to side and flick your tongue.

The fireflies bounded and bounced until a picture of a rabbit appeared. Excited bunnies thumped at the foot of the silver birch tree.

Fenix knew the last firework depended on a light shining from the tippy top of the tree.

With a renewed burst of speed, the little bug pushed off, soared above the other fireflies, and held onto a leaf swaying gently in the breeze.

On cue, Fenix's light joined the others'.

Practice your bunny jumps again. Then, lift a foot and stomp it on the ground a few times.

Pretend to be a leaf holding onto the branch and swaying gently.

Fenix looked down to see the shape the Fliers had formed and laughed with delight.

The crowd yipped and hooted. Everyone agreed fireflies were the perfect *Spirit of the Season*.

One voice rose above the rest. "Way to go, Fenix!" called Bolt. "The most daring Firework Flier that ever was!"

Make some celebratory noises and cheerful appreciations. Do you find you want to jump around?

Thee end!
The end.

(My grandpa always ended stories this way, and I like to share the fun.)

Thanks for being my dance partner.

Until our next adventure,

Love,

Konora

We're Waiting for Your Feedback

ONCE UPON A DANCE is a mother-daughter collaboration.

We check for reviews daily and would be immensely grateful for a kind, honest review on Amazon or Goodreads, or a shout-out on social media.

@Once_UponADance

Konora

Optional Classroom Extension
Pretend you're a firefly who is part of the Firework Fliers. Work together to create a picture. Some starting ideas:
- the first letter of your school or studio
- the ages of participants, for example a seven and an eight
- a smiley face
- a star, rectangle, or circle

See how many fun food shapes you can create. Some starting ideas:
- an apple
- an ice cream cone
- a carrot
- a burger bun
- a piece of cake
- a cookie
- broccoli

Teamwork is one theme of this book, and you can use the story to introduce any sort of team-building exercise. Some starting ideas:
- Cross the river to get to the Solstice Celebration: Challenge kids to work together to cross an imaginary river using items distributed among the students, such as paper plates, hula hoops, or ropes. Encourage the kids to plan how to use the items without touching a river made from tape, a scarf, blanket, etc.
- Balance a plate of food. In teams, see how many objects will stack on a plate.
- Play telephone with a list of animals.

Feel free to tag @Once_UponADance with your activities or ideas!

Dance-It-Out! Stories

AGES 4+

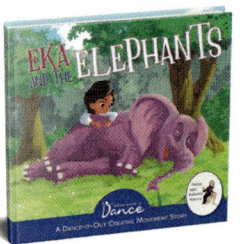 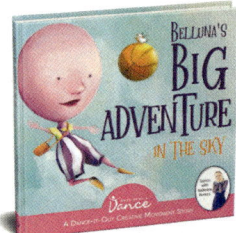 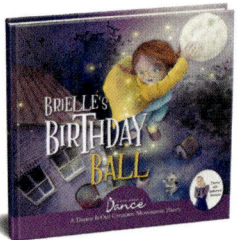 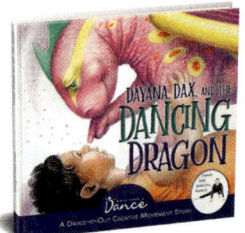 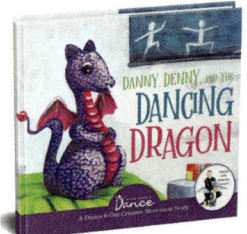

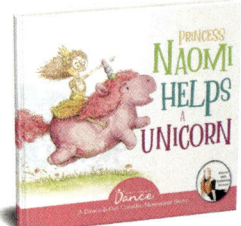 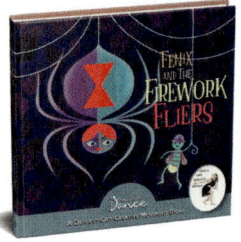 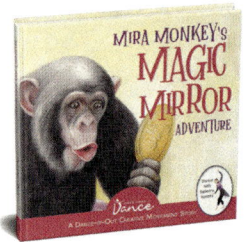 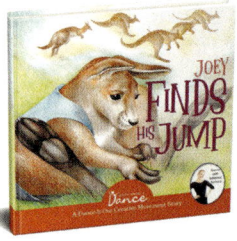 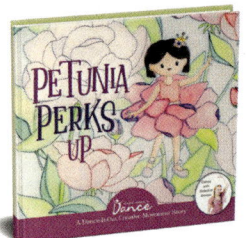

AGES 5+

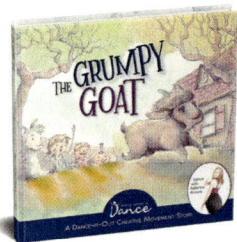  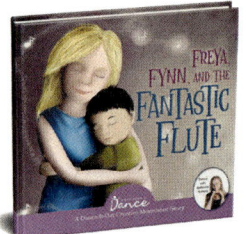 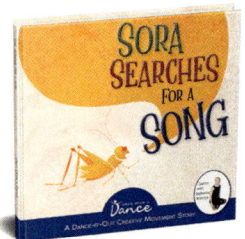 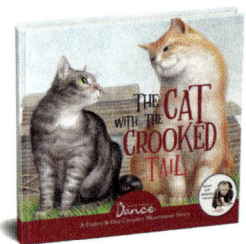

AGES 6+

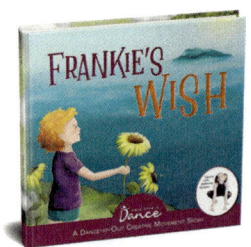 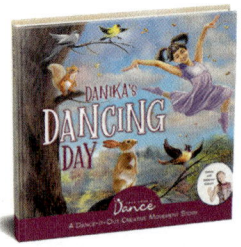 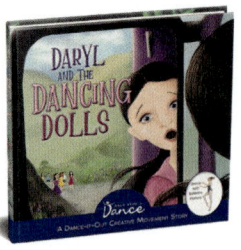 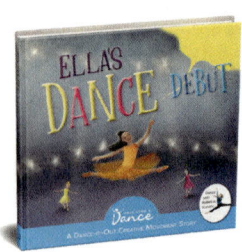 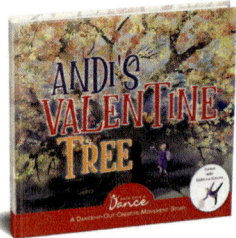

Other Series by Once Upon a Dance

AGES 6+

  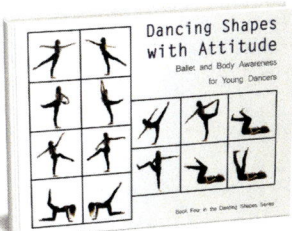 

AGES 8+

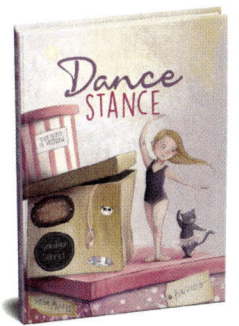 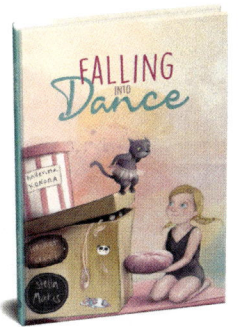 

Made in the USA
Middletown, DE
27 July 2024